OUR PRESIDENT: BILL CLINTON

by Shelley Bedik

SCHOLASTIC INC.

New York Toronto London Auckland Sydney

For Bill, Sasha, Max, and Aaron — and Lucy and Daisy, of course!

Photo Credits
Front Cover © 1993 Owen D. B./Black Star.
Back Cover: (left) © Arkansas Gazette/SIPA Press; (right) © Ira Wyman/SYGMA.

pp 3 and 29: © Ralf Finn Hestoft/SABA Press; pp 5 and 11: © Arkansas Gazette/SIPA Press; p 7: Courtesy of Clinton Presidential Campaign; p 9: © SYGMA Photo News; pp 13, 19, 31: © AP/Wide World Photos; pp 15 and 25: © Bob McNeely; p 17: © Ron Haviv/SABA Press; pp 21, 23, 32: © Robert Trippett/SIPA Press; p 25: © James Colburn/PhotoReporters; p 26: Nina Berman/SIPA Press; p 27: © Cynthia Johnson/Gamma Liaison; p 28: © Steve Liss/SABA Press.

ISBN 0-590-06649-8

12 11 10 9 8 7 6 5 4 3 2 1

7 8 9/9 0 1 2/0

Printed in the U.S.A.

24

First Scholastic printing, January 1997

  Bill Clinton was born in 1946. He grew up in a small town called Hope, Arkansas. When Bill was a young boy, Hope was the kind of place where everyone knew everyone else. People didn't lock their doors at night. Everyone felt very safe there.

☆

Three months before he was born, something very sad happened to his family. His father died in a bad car accident. So Bill lived with his grandparents while his mother went to school to become a nurse.

Bill when he was about 1½ years old.

Bill's grandmother believed that education was very important. She read to him all the time. She even hung cards around his high chair to help him learn numbers. She did a good job teaching Bill. He could read when he was only three years old!

Bill's mother married for the second time. The family moved to a new town, Hot Springs. Soon Bill had a new little brother.

Bill, his mother, and his half brother, Roger.

When Bill was a teenager,
he was an important leader in
his high school and church.
He got good grades and
worked hard to help people
in his community. Bill worked
hard at something else, too.
He practiced his saxophone
until he played so well that
he won first place in a band
contest!

Bill is in the first row on the far left.

One summer, Bill was chosen to be part of Boy's Nation. He met many other kids who were interested in leadership and the government.

That summer, he met the person who was then the leader of the whole country. He shook hands with John F. Kennedy, the President of the United States! Bill's mother says, "That's when I knew Bill would grow up to be in government."

Bill Clinton shakes hands with President John F. Kennedy.

Bill thought he might want to become a doctor. Then he thought he would make his living playing the saxophone. Instead, he decided to go to Georgetown University in Washington, D.C.

When he finished college, he won a big honor. He was chosen to go to a school in England to study.

Bill Clinton still plays the saxophone for fun.

☆

When he came back to the United States, Bill started law school. He knew that he wanted to become a lawyer. He also knew that he wanted to return to Arkansas. He says, "All I wanted to do was go home. I thought I would start my law practice in Hot Springs and see if I could run for office."

During his first campaign in 1992, Bill Clinton stayed in touch with people by holding meetings in small towns.

When Bill was in law school, he met someone he thought was very special. Her name was Hillary Rodham. She was a lawyer, too.

Once, Bill and Hillary were taking a drive. Hillary saw a house she thought looked nice. Just a short while after that drive, Bill said, "Hillary, I bought the house you liked. So you'd better marry me. I can't live there by myself." And Hillary said yes!

Three years later, Bill was elected governor of Arkansas. He spent most of the next fourteen years trying to make education, health care, and the environment better in his state. He wanted more jobs and better roads for the people in Arkansas.

Governor Clinton and Hillary attend a special dinner at the White House.

In 1980, Bill and Hillary had a daughter. Bill says, "I was there when Chelsea was born. It was the most incredible thing I've ever been through."

Now Chelsea is a teenager. She says, "My parents taught me to think for myself. And they taught me to treat other people the way you would want to be treated yourself." She thinks her mom and dad are great!

Hillary, Bill, and Chelsea celebrate
during Election '92.

So do lots of other people. In 1992, they voted
to make Chelsea's father the President of the
United States! American voters felt Bill Clinton
did such a good job during his four-year term as
President that he was reelected in 1996!

President Clinton campaigning in 1996.

President Clinton takes time to visit towns all across the country, especially if there has been an emergency or a big storm.

He has worked hard to pass laws that keep the air
we breathe and the water we drink safe. He cares
about the environment and Americans' health.

He has helped grown-ups find better jobs. He makes sure that families get the health care they need.

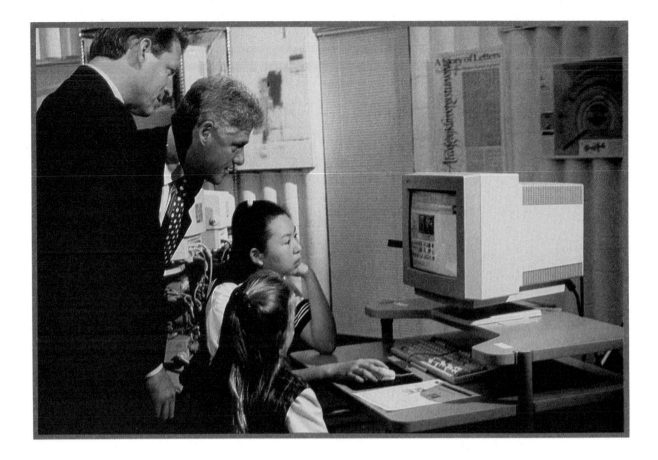

   President Clinton thinks education is very important. He wants all classrooms to have computers, and has worked hard to make sure school is a fun, safe place for kids.

As our forty-second
President, Bill Clinton lives
in the White House in
Washington, D.C. That's a
long way from his first home
in Hope, Arkansas. But Bill
Clinton thinks it's the right
place for him to be. That's
where he can do the work
he always dreamed of.

President Bill Clinton and Vice President Al Gore will work together to keep our country strong and safe, and to make our planet healthy.

President Clinton, Chelsea, and Hillary Clinton with the Vice President's family: son Albert Gore III, daughter Sarah, and Tipper and Al Gore.